Professor M.R. Ali

Poems *for* Art's Sake

MULTIMEDIA PUBLISHING

Poems for Art's Sake

Published by:
Multimedia Publishing, Artology International
The Chalet House, Golf Club Road
St. George's Hill, Weybridge, Surrey KT13 ONN, England

Cover: Jukka Setälä
Layout: Liisa Valkama

British Library cataloguing in publication data.
A Catalogue record for this book available from the British Library.

Printed in Hong Kong 1997

ISBN 1 899873 01 5

I

Art through Poems

INTRODUCTION

Art is what you see and poems are what you hear.
Put them together, what do you get? A new direction
in imagination! Poems bring life into art, while art
starts emerging as the laurel of poems.

Such a combination with its fascination is a great
temptation for a new literary creation.

What you are going to read is not a new poetic breed,
but an attempt to take poetry of the present day
into the journey of tomorrow.

The art is now seen through the poet's eyes, colour-
ed with all shades and shadows to portray art
movements, from Primitive, Renaissance, Cubism,
Surrealism, Minimalism, Graffiti, to Installation
and so on, with the majestic touch they deserve.

After all, poems and art are about feelings and
emotions that make your blood pulsate and your
heart beat with every word you hear and every picture
you see.

For art's sake let us now take the poetry to its wake
and see what limits it can break!

12

Painting 1

Primitive Art

Primitive Art
    Is never surpassed,
        So they say.

Primitive Art
    Is everywhere,
        And here to stay.

Primitive Art
    Came from far away,
        And did not lose its way.

The primitive artist
    Is master of reality,
        With intense creativity.

The primitive artist
    Is a child of nature,
        Reflecting its simplicity.

The primitive artist
    Has the wit, the magic,
        And the popularity.

Renaissance Art

The mystique of the Renaissance
Was renounced for an age that gave
The giving and the gift of thinking.

Up and up and up
There came
The age of enlightenment
From the middle ages darkness.

Opening the doors of learning,
Shining with wisdom and knowledge,
To encourage a new era of advancement
Replacing the early ignorance.

A welcome to the cycle of fortune,
Driven by art and science
On the road of tomorrow.

The new birth on earth,
Worth the waiting.
Giving power to humanity,
The people needed a new reality.

In every direction,
Together they emerged
Victors in every sector.

Architecture, painting and sculpture
Were the order
To serve a new civilization.

Without warning
Medici and Leonardo were born,
Angelo and Rafaello were adorned,
And so on and so on.

Men, women and children,
In their dozens,
Grew accustomed
To the fallen blessing from heaven.

Able peers with armies of volunteers
Looking at the reawakening,
Searching for perfection.

The Renaissance progress,
As an avalanche with no match,
Swept the masses of all classes.

The artists and the scientists,
As prime movers
Of resurgence in excellence,

Grew in influence,
Marching in success
As a non stop chain reaction.

In the rebirth
Dawned a new horizon
In literature and culture.

The unprecedented revolution
In inventions and discoveries,
In thoughts and actions,
Generated great
Artistic inspiration.

From a revolution to a movement,
The cycle of learning and thinking
Enlarged beyond recognition.

Now the human endeavours
Had a new conquest.
The Renaissance Art
Manifested a new confidence
In the ability of man.

Impressionism

Olé Olé, Renoir and Monet
On a sunny day
Moved in the open
To paint and to play.

With others they discovered
The spontaneous touch
Of light and colours.

They admired every scene
On the banks of the Seine.
They captured
Every moment in time.
Every painting became
A vision in rhyme.
A prime experiment
For Impressionists was meant.
Olé Olé.

All Impressionists
Felt happy and gay
For discovering a new
Beautiful way.

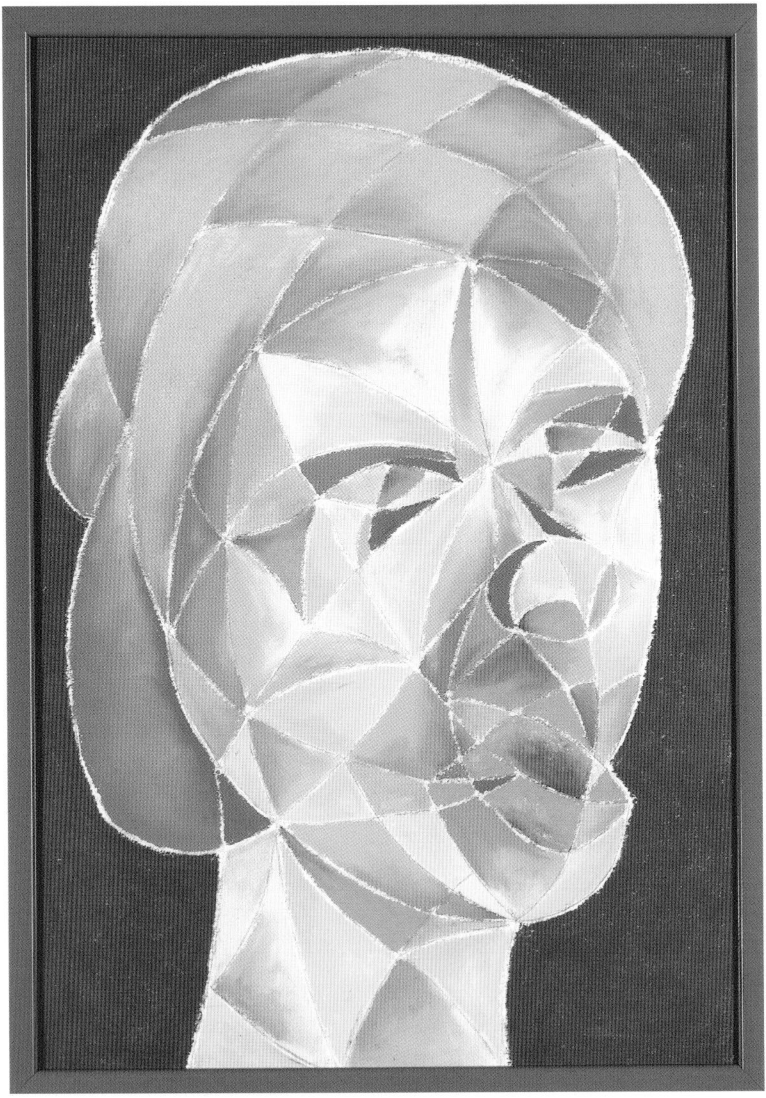

Painting 2

Expressionism

What a block
Was Van Gogh
Who rocked
The art world amok.

He knocked and broke
The rules of reality
To express his insanity
In unprecendented clarity.

Expressionists love distortion.
They see it through emotion
As a new art dimension,
Culminating from inner vision.

Heightened by deliberate protesting
And strong colours,
It is the message, not the rules,
That rules.

Van Gogh was not a fool,
He set the modern art school.

Fauvism

FAUV — FAUV —
Donatello among the beasts,
It is the feast of artistes.

All that matters is flat colours,
Contrasting with each other.

In a new style of painting
Reflecting the mood of happening.

Fauvism as a beast was born,
Into an art movement has grown.

Cubism

The cube is a cup of Cubism
And the vase of blossom,
That sends ripples and rhythm
To the art world of mystery'ism.

Picasso drank from the cup of the cube
Using his mouth, not a tube,
Sucking new ideas from the woman's boob.

Now the cube faces
Crises in all places.
Picasso deserted the ace of aces
To let Hockney pick up the traces.

Figurative

FIG FIG IS FIGURATIVE !

Painting 4

Abstract

25

TACT TACT IS ABSTRACT!

Dadaism

Dada wanted to be
A war conscious refugee,

With new avant-garde art
And a manifesto to start.

A work of nihilistic gesture
As a movement for the future.

Zürich was chosen as a centre.
Provocations became the order.

Dada left mama behind,
So Dadaism he could find.

Surrealism

Fill me with a feeling
To give my life a meaning!
Applause me with a smile,
We love each other's style.

Please jump into my pocket
So I can take off my jacket.
Soon we'll play our cricket;
The broom is a bat and the ball is a bucket.

Hold my lung with your tongue
And give me a kiss with a big bang.
I am just a punk
Looking for my funk.

Encourage me with your courage,
Marry me with your marriage,
And massage me with your message.
Now you deserve the privilege!

Painting 5

Dress me Scottish
and look at me as you wish.
To wash or to dish,
Now you know I am a bird not a fish.

Back where we have started
To join the people before they parted.
Making fun of ourselves
Makes us happy, not down hearted.

Believe it or not
To surrealize a poem is fun,
To twist and to squeeze the son of a gun,
I can say well done.

Minimalism

To minimize and not compromise
Is the art of minimalists.
The less, the more
Is the wisdom
Behind minimalist freedom.

To simplify, to magnify,
That is why
Everybody can try
To paint and decorate
In a simple way.

You may paint a picture in white
And you will be right
To win the fight,
As long as the critics are quiet.

You can also have simple living,
Decorating your house with nothing.
Who cares if you have a bed or no bed,
Or sleep on the floor instead,
Or have a chair to sit on,
As long as you go on
Having little dress,
No excess.
Just simple
Is ample.

Pop Art

Pop Pop popular,
Pop art is forever.

Andy Warhol and others
Worked together as brothers

To manifest the quest
For the materialistic conquest,

A vernacular culture
With mass consumer flavour,

Shared by artistic professionals,
From nationals to internationals.

Painting 6

Graffiti

Here, ———————— there
And everywhere,
Dancing letters
With vivid colours.

All you see is the magic scene
That yesterday had not been.
You wonder how it all came about,
This devout art without doubt.

The art of graffiti grew
From the poor and the few
As a code of communication
Spreading fast in fascination.

That is why graffiti refuses entry
Into any museum or gallery.
It loves to stay outside
In keeping with its pride.

Graffiti is not advertising,
And it is not politicizing.
It is the status quo criticizer,
And the establishment antagonizer.

It is not surprising,
Graffiti needs no legitimizing
As art on the wall,
Setting the goal for all.

Deltaism

You flying delta
With many meanings,
Created for all concepts
With mathematical leanings.

You flying delta
With scientific wings,
Small in appearance,
Strong as the Sphinx.

The creation of Sir Isaac
Who desired you should be
The guiding symbol
Of new discovery.

Indeed he succeeded
In making you queen.
Without you new discoveries
Would not have been.

To conquer other places,
Leaving no sanctuary
For science and art
And all technology.

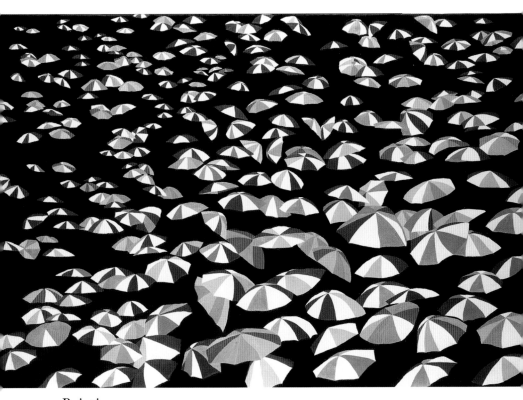

Painting 7

You move at the speed of light
As in relativity,
And race into quantum mechanics
And all its activity.

Touching grand unification
With no time for adulation,
You busy delta,
Give us time for inspiration.

Now be my flying delta
With artistic wings,
Landing on the art world,
Show me what you can bring.

To create a concept
Based on my artistic rhythm,
From you, the delta,
I found Deltaism.

Fractal Art

Self similar

A son and a father,

A daughter and a mother.

Geometry of nature,

A galaxy's structure,

Mountains and moreover

Clouds and under

The chaos and the order

All together,

In general,

Are the Art of Fractal.

Installation

Installation is the art of imagination,
The creation of desired orientation,
The deception of space and location,
The falsification of the sensation.

All in all
Is what to install,
On the floor
Or on the wall.
Everybody has his goal.

Installation is not decoration.
Installation is not presentation.
Installation is not examination.
Installation is manifestation.

To manifest the possible,
And the impossible.
To install the visible,
And the invisible.

For example:
Manifesting the moon as the offspring of the sun,
What fun.
Or manifesting Venus as the step-sister of Mars,
What a farce.

Another example:
Manifesting the mystery of memory
In poetry or in pottery,
In geometry or in mockery,
In February or in January,
Auxiliary or subsidiary,
All that matters is that
The manifestation is part of the Installation.

Take more examples:
Installing the usables and the disposables;
Installing this on that;
Installing the head in the hat;
Installing the cat as a king rat;
What are you looking at?

42 What about the following example,
As the last sample:
Dealing with the touchables and the untouchables,
The miserables and the horribles.
Do their ghosts and souls need manifestations
In invisible installations?

In conclusion
Let us say
The best Installation in some occasion
Has no explanation,
It's just born out of frustration.

PART TWO

2

Poems of Artists

INTRODUCTION

Imagine T.S. Eliot and Pablo Picasso were commissioned to do an unusual piece of work. The first to make a poem about the second, the second to make a painting of the first.

If we went on further in our imagination we could ask Eliot and Picasso to extend their good work to Ludwig Beethoven, Henry Moore, Elvis Presley and Rudolf Nureyev, and to include as well an actor, a clown, a designer, a photographer and a writer, all of their own choice.

To complete this commission we would ask Eliot and Picasso to make a poem and a painting respectively of themselves.

The finale would be a magnificent collection of eleven paintings of various artists with their corresponding poems.

The public would then see how a silent painting of an artist is enhanced by its spoken poem. The poems, all of a sudden, animate each artist into life. That is what poems of artists are all about!

46

The Actor

Acting, reacting,
Casting, blasting,
Raving, craving,
Biting, fighting,
Sporting, courting,
Sitting, picketing,
Upsetting, blood-letting,
Fascinating, discriminating,
Hesitating, accommodating,
Astonishing, perishing,
Convincing, unconvincing,
Kissing, promising,
Dressing, depressing,
Flavouring, unwavering,
Wandering, suffering,
Murmuring, flattering,
Alluring, enduring,
Boring, roaring,
Firing, inspiring,
Aspiring, tiring,
Hearing, talking,
Daring, overbearing,
Weeping, laughing,
Singing, swinging,
Sickening, maddening,
Opening, fastening,
Gunning, running,

Farming, alarming,
Burning, learning,
Churning, concerning,
Entertaining, performing,
Blooming, assuming,
Seeming, redeeming.
And many, many more,
As roles to adore,
To adopt or to ignore,
As stories to explore.

The actor
Is a grand master
Of becoming another character,
A malefactor or benefactor.

Casts of actors are numerous.
Some actors prefer the serious,
Some like the dubious.
But the humour is fabulous.

A good actor needs voice, emotion,
Style and body motion,
To express his role with fascination,
To attract applause and admiration.

To a certain extent
All of us act and pretend,
Wearing the garments of a saint
Or playing the fool with a friend.

Public acting is not new,
And performing is not taboo.
For politicians it grew
As a job they love to do.

That is why actors
Are needed all over
As modern protectors
In art, in business, and moreover.

Actors for rent or for sale
Are handy, trendy to hail.
They can tell any tale,
And can wear any veil.

But as an actor
Dressing in the skin of another,
Is it bliss,
Or is it a curse
To be someone else?

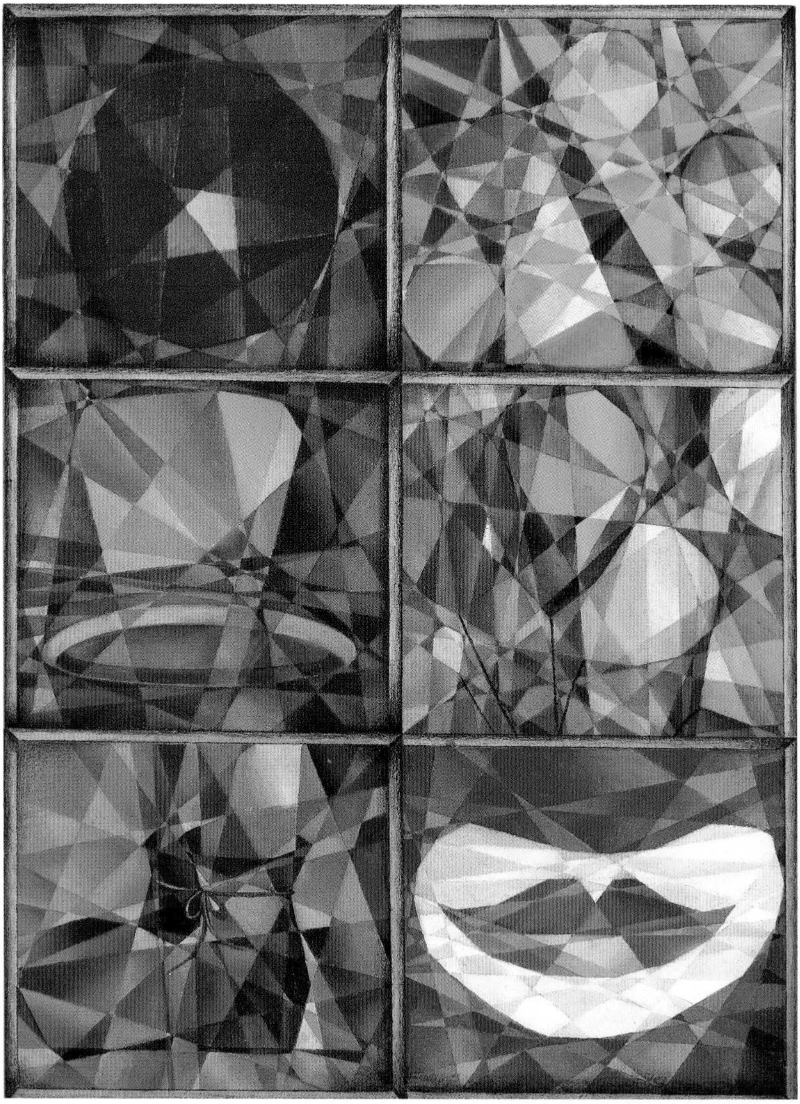

Painting 10

The Clown

Laugh and laughter
Clown and jester
Just enter the world of laughter

Wear your mood upside down
Wear your jacket inside out

Tear and wear your feeling
Laugh the night away
And live a happy day
Say what you like to say

Just enter the world of laughter
With your mood like a clown and jester
With your face upside down
Like a clown

Laugh and laugh

The Composer

Symphony in Red

    Accordion – lively, brisk
    Banjo – very fast
    Cello – extremely soft, mute
    Clarinet – dying away gradually
    Drum – loud, louder
    Flute – flowing tender
    Fiddle – from the beginning
    Guitar – loving, emotional
    Harp – majestic, soft, delicate
    Horn – in hunting style
    Lyre – sweet
    Mandolin – fast
    Organ – sad, mournful
    Piano – attack; continue without a pause
    Rebab – comic
    Saxophone – agitated
    Tambourine – effortless; in a free manner
    Trumpet – vigorous
    Ud – final part of the movement
    Viola – warm.

        Now the red symphony is conducted.
        The composition is orchestrated.
        The work is musingly completed.
        So our dear composer has indicated!

The Dancer

In a trance
I dance
Dancing is my prance
To enhance my chance
of my body feeling ——

In a trance
I dance
With a glance
Dancing is a romance
And a body healing ——

In a trance
I dance
Like a lance
Thrown in an expanse
Like a body piercing ——

In a trance
I dance
To advance
And to enhance
My soul seeking

The Designer

Good taste is good design.
That is fine!
What makes the design shine?
When it hits the headlines.
Then it is a good sign
For the designing artist,
Who is also an applied scientist,
To harness his harvest
With wit and a twist of the wrist,
With unbeatable zest.

He can be a stylist,
He can be an analyst,
He can be an ergonomist,
Producing an impressive list
Of modern products that exist.

As he is an idealist,
The designer
Is a path-finder
And an innovator,
Serving the consumer
As his brother,
And he is an admirer
Of mother nature.

The Painter

When the painter's eye
Starts seeking
To arrest
The right moment,

Like a hunter
Who is waiting
For the prey
He is wanting,

Or an eagle
From above,
Looking down
To his love,

Or a captain
In stormy weather,
Looking forward
To the harbour,

Or a soldier
Searching hard
For a target
On the map.

When the painter's eye
Starts mixing
All the colours,
All the forms,

It is the moment
To remember
Every form is the norm
Of the artist's brainstorm,

And to remember
All colours
Stand better
When they need each other.

When the scene needs a green
And the flower craves a yellow,
Then the cottage needs a shade
And the tree begs a shadow.

With the final touch,
All forms and colours
Stand together
As pals forever.

When the painter's eye
Starts searching
For an aim
To his vision,

Like a child
In search
For his toy
Or his mother,

Or a teacher
Lost in thought,
Working hard
Through his notes.

From Leonardo
To Picasso,
From the isms
Of early times,

All painters
Passing barriers,
Aiming higher
And higher.

Then the painter's eye
Finds the answer.

The Photographer

An artist in particular,
An explorer in nature,
The camera is his lover.
That is why he is popular
As a visual demonstrator,
Putting everything together
As the news breaker,
Art commentator,
Scientific discoverer,
And events recorder.

He is everywhere
And in every corner.
Like an intelligent tiger,
Ardent to be the victor
In a game of adventure.
He is a candid observer.
Of human behaviour.

He is also a storyteller;
The story is told with a picture
Of an assassinated leader,
Or injured player.

He loves the flower
As subject matter.
But it doesn't matter.
With his finger
On the shutter,
He can capture
Any exposure,
From a movie thriller
To a grand spectacular.
Giving pleasure
To his viewer
Is what he can offer.

He is a day-dreamer
Dreaming of being a winner
Of the honour,
Of being first, not a loser.
That is why he is a researcher
And astrologer.

With the camera and its visual power

He can look deeper and deeper
Into tiny atomic structure,
Further and further
Into outer space and its wonder.

To feel better
He looks in his mirror
To find the answer
To how long he should wander
In the world of never never,
To ride the danger,
And to cross over
Any border
To capture his flying saucer!

The Poet

The poet is his master's voice
And the people's choice.
I am the poet.

I say what you like to hear.
I say what others fear.
I say it loud and clear.
I say it right in your ear.
I am the poet.

If you like what I say,
If you say that you may,
If you like it that way,
Then you say every day,
'I am the poet'.

I speak for all occasions,
Peace, war and celebrations.
I speak for all generations
And all denominations.
I am the poet.

A friend to the poor and rich
And the son of a bitch.
I like to tease the witch
When she is in my ditch.
I am the poet.

My poetic justice
Is revenge to the thankless.
My poetic licence
Is a kiss of conscience.
I am the poet.

"When you see me coming
Step aside.
A lot of men didn't
A lot of men died."
I am the poet.

The birds have sung.
The old and the young
Have joyfully swung
To poetry of every tongue.
I am the poet.

One poet is a laureate;
The second with unknown fate;
The third is not that great;
The fourth his words, he ate.
I am the poet.

Epics are a rarity,
Lyrics are beauty,
An ode to duty,
The ditty is always witty.
I am the poet.

To know what I write
Is for you,
And to know what I say
Is true.
I am the poet.

The deaf and the blind
Have peace of mind
When they find
They are poets in kind.
I am the poet.

Every poem is an equation
Of feelings and emotion,
Love and devotion,
Hate and frustration.
I am the poet.

My self-portrait
Drawn with a word palette
As a masterpiece of spirit,
Exhibited in public and private.
I am the poet.

I take my flying carpet
On a lunar transit.
I blow my trumpet
When around Jupiter I orbit.
I am the poet.

I am the literary bandit,
That is my gift.
When others quit,
My poems fit.
That's it.

The Sculptor

Sculpt me like an angel,
Sculpt me like a devil.
Sculpt me with a long nose,
Holding in my big ear a red rose.
Sculpt me like a squirrel,
Happily sleeping in a cradle.
Sculpt me like a hero in battle,
Or a statue of a saint in a temple.
Sculpt me like a champ receiving a medal,
Or a hell's angel on a motorcycle.
Sculpt me like your double,
Because I love to be your model.
Now you are sculpting a puzzle.

The Singer

The singer sings songs
Of love, sadness and sorrow,
The singer brings gigs
To brighten a rainy tomorrow.

The singer's sweet voice
When it becomes the listeners' choice
Is a treat for a broken heart.

A song for listening,
A song for relaxing,
A song for romancing,
And a song for dancing.
All songs are for a reason
And every song for a season.

The voice power of a singer
Makes us quiver
And gives us a thrill and wonder
If the singer is a stranger.

Let us together stand
Holding hand and hand,
On top of the world;
The following song we uphold:

"We sing a love song for you ——
And if you want us to ——
We'll send it with a kiss or two ——
To show our feelings are true ——

Let our song outdo ——
Any song we knew ——
Let it be our debut ——"

The Writer

Write me a story
Of my past glory.

Write me a book
On how I look.

Write me a play
On how I act and sway.

Write for me a tale
On how I escape from hell.

Write for me an article
On my adventures in the jungle.

Write for me a song,
Tell me to whom I belong.

Write for me a fiction
On my obsession and addiction.

Write my biography.
Don't make it a catastrophe.

Thank you for your writing.

PART THREE

3

Word Poems

INTRODUCTION

A word needs a verse,

a verse needs a poem,
and a poem needs a story.

Why?

Each word has travelled in time to gain some mean-ing. It has a history. It is a story in its own right. It therefore deserves a poem.

Fourteen words have been chosen, from apple to zero. Each word is light-heartedly or seriously con-sidered as subject-matter for an unusual type of poem.

While I was exploring each word's strength in playing a role in the poetry world, I became more and more amazed by the countless possibilities.

The concept of word poems is the unique re-presentation of words within words. The effectiveness of such a combination can be summed up as – "Words cut more than swords!"

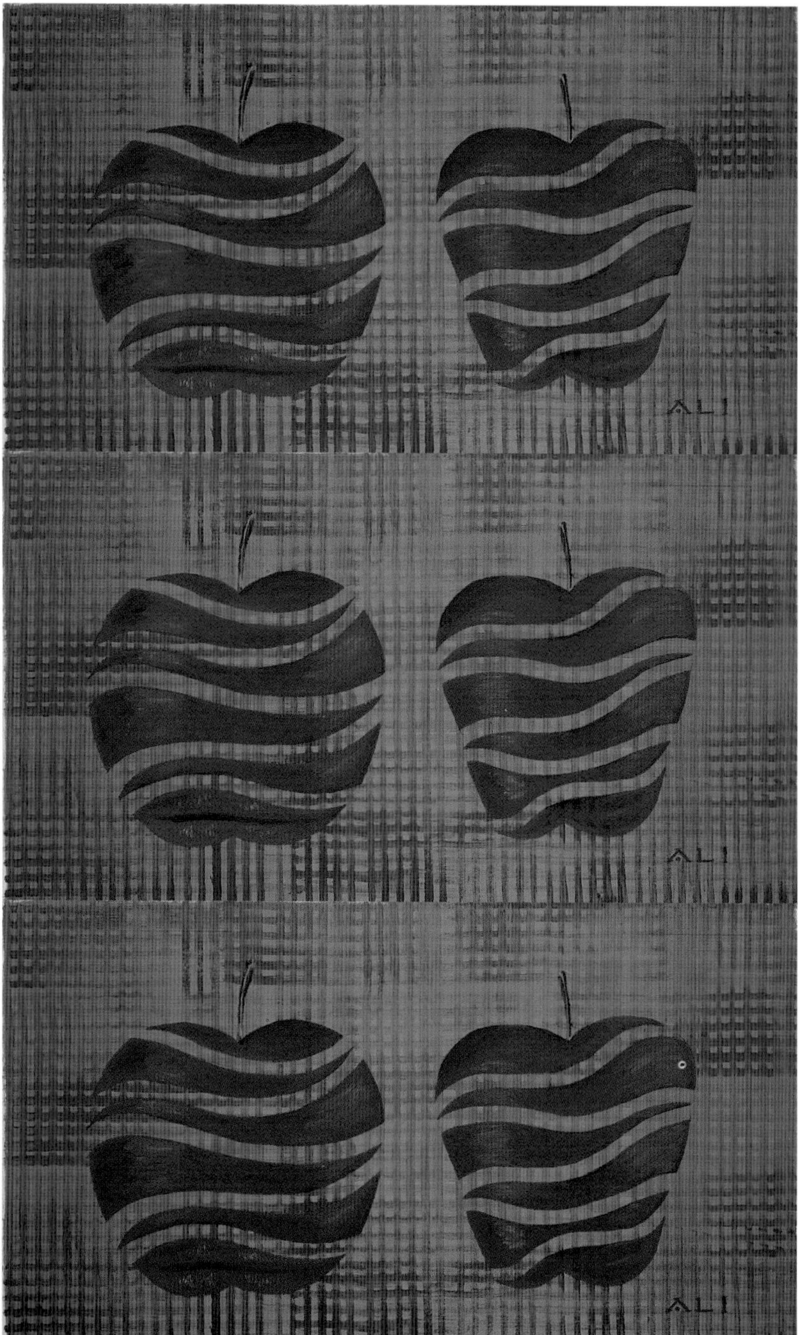

Painting 16

Apples

Apple,	Apple,	Apple,	Apple	&	Apple
Appl,	Appl,	Appl,	Appl	&	Appl
Apple,	Appla,	Appli,	Applo	&	Applu
Apple,	Apple,	Apple,	Apple	&	Apple
Pple,	Pple,	Pple,	Pple	&	Pple
Apple,	Epple,	Ipple,	Opple	&	Upple
Apple,	Apple	Apple,	Apple	&	Apple
Apaple,	Apeple,	Apiple,	Apople	&	Apuple

Now we have:

Apple   the   Apple
Apple   the   Paple
Apple   the   Peple
Apple   the   Piple
Apple   the   Pople
Apple   the   Puple

All are sorts of clones of Apples

Boy

What a boy.
What a joy.
    He is fun
    He is son,
    He is the only one
    Under the sun!   What a boy.
                       What a joy.
             To his parents
             He is savant.
             In school, he is brilliant.
             To his friends, he is vibrant.
What a boy.
What a joy.
    To his sister,
    He is mister,
    Not a master
    Or protester.   What a boy.
                       What a joy.
             With his teachers
             He endeavours,
             And nurtures
             All lectures.
What a boy.
What a joy.
    He tends
    To blend
    With his friends
    To discuss all trends.

I

I laugh
And I cry.
I live
And I die.

        I and I
        Are more than I.
        I for spring,
        I for summer,
        I for autumn,
        I for winter.

                I and I
                Are more than I.
                I for you,
                I for him,
                I for her,
                I for them.

I and I
Are more than I.
I for the truth,
I for the lie,
I for the smile,
I for the sigh.

        I and I
        Are more than I.
        I say hello,
     Another I says goodbye.
   How many I's are in one I?
      You cannot deny
   You and I are full of I's.

OK

OK IS ALL RIGHT

ALL RIGHT IS OK

OK IS ALL RIGHT

OK IS OK

OK IS OK

OK IS OK

OK

OK

OK

OK IS ALL RIGHT

THEN WHAT IS WRONG ?!

The Pillow

I am the pillow under your head,
I am your friend, don't be afraid.
Good morning, for a day lies ahead.

Dear fellow,
Say hello to your pillow
And good luck to follow.

I am the pillow in waiting,
I am the pillow on your bed,
I am the pillow of comfort,
Please stop thinking and sleep instead.

Dear fellow,
Say good night to your pillow
And sweet dreams to follow.

Painting 17

Rabbit

Who will change a rabbit for a rat?
Or have them both – rat and rabbit?
They cohabit and get married
To breed a small rarebit!

A genetic miracle
Of the scientific pinnacle!
Engineered in an experiment
To conceive a rare infant.

The newly wed couple
Living on the pebble,
The mother happily pregnant
And the father fearfully silent.

The dominant factor
Mingled with its counter
Resulted in a little twinkle
Like Tarzan in the jungle.

Now the offspring
Can easily fling
In any race of grace,
Beating any horse on any course.

Inherited from the father
The rat racer
And from the mother
The nuclear fast breeder.

The young new creature
With lovely features
Was christened Lam Lam
Without kalam.

The super Lam Lam
Tamam tamam
Agreed with all honesty
To sponsor the rabbit charity.

The father rat
Put on a red hat,
Displeased with Lam Lam
Without kalam.

The poor Lam Lam
Said haram haram,
Changed his mind,
No excuse he could find.

The mother rabbit
And the father rat
Have the habit
Of blaming the rarebit.

Soon the rarebit,
Bit by bit,
Won the race at Ascot
As the Queen's mascot.

The rarebit was decorated
And a life peer was created
As Lord Lam Lam
Without kalam.

Now he is a dream
Of the realm
And the dream of Ahlam
Without kalam.

Lord Lam Lam
Became a dream num num
Of every charity
In the whole community.

We, all of us, are jubilant
Of this excellent experiment.
Ten cheers for the first family
Of Lam Lam
Without kalam.

SHIPS

SHĬP..
SHĬP SHĬP..
SHÎP SHÎP...
SH̄ĪP . SH̄ĪP . SH̄ĪP..
SHIP SHIP . SHIP SHIP..
SH̄ĪP .. SH̄ĪP .. SH̄ĪP .. SHĬP SHĬP SHĬP .. SHĬP..
SHÎP .. SHÎP .. SHÎP .. SHÎP .. SHÎP..
SHIP .. SHIP .. SHIP .. SHIP..
SH̄ĪP .. SH̄ĪP .. SH̄ĪP..
SHĬP ... SHĬP ... SHĬP..
SH̄ĪP ... SH̄ĪP ... SH̄ĪP..
SHÎP SHÎP .. SHIP SHIP..
SHÎP .. SHÎP .. SHÎP..
SHĬP ... SHĬP..
SH̄ĪP .. SH̄ĪP..
SHÎP SHIP..
SHIP SHIP..
AND MANŶ
SHĬP̄S̄.

Loudness ˇ ˆ
Word length – – –
Word spacing . . .
Number of ships 53

TAKE

88

Take out the   E

"   "   "   K

"   "   "   A

"   "   "   T

"   "   "   E

"   "   "   K

"   "   "   A

"   "   "   T

How many   TAKES
Have you   TAKEN?

Trees

Trees, trees dancing in the breeze
Trees, trees swinging at ease
    Trees, please, give me your ears.

Trees, trees standing everywhere
Looking and watching in despair
    Trees, please, give me your ears.

Trees, trees I know your fears
Trees, trees wipe out your tears
    Trees, please, give me your ears.

All trees are blessed, we confess
Each one is a holy tree and a princess
    Trees, please, give me your ears.

Trees, truly you have served mankind

In his need, in his conquest and in his find
    Trees, please, give me your ears.

On Christmas day and with the Christmas tree
Celebrating together as one family
    Trees, please, give me your ears.

Now be happy, dance and sway
Celebrating with others your tree day
    Trees, please, give me your ears.

Cheers without fears our dears
For many fruitful years
    Trees, please, dance and close your ears.

Painting 20

UNDER

UNDER
     UNDER
          UNDER
               UNDER
                    UNDER
                    OVER
               OVER
          OVER
     OVER
OVER
UNDER   OVER
     UNDER   OVER
        UNDER OVER
     OVER   UNDER
OVER   UNDER

     UNDER & OVER
     UNDER & OVER
      OVER & UNDER
      OVER & UNDER
      OVER & UNDER

What is UNDER? Maybe WATER!

What is OVER? Maybe WATER!

WATER is UNDER and WATER is OVER

– That is the answer!!

VICTORY

VEE	FOR	VICTORY
VIC	VIC	VIC

VEE	FOR	VICTORY
VIC	VIC	VIC

VEE	FOR	VICTORY
VIC	VIC	VIC

VEE	FOR	VICTORY
VIC	VIC	VIC

VEE	FOR	VICTORY
VIC	VIC	VIC

VIC	FOR	THE	VICTOR
SHIT	FOR	THE	LOSER

Wow!

The know-how, somehow,
Is to allow 5 seconds
To read Wow, Wow, Wow.
If you pass the test
You are Wow, Wow, Wow!

Wow	Wow	Wow
Wee	Wee	Wee
Woo	Woo	Woo
Wow	Wee	Wee
Wow	Woo	Woo
Wow	Wee	Woo
Wee	Wow	Wow
Wee	Woo	Woo
Wee	Wow	Woo
Woo	Wow	Wow
Woo	Wee	Wee
Woo	Wow	Wee

Yellow

I love yellow
My face is yellow
My hands are yellow
My shirt is yellow
My shoes are yellow
My car is yellow
My dreams are yellow
My paper is yellow
My friends are yellow
My tongue is yellow
I love yellow
I am yellow
I am yellow man
Looking for yellow woman!

Zero

The Big Bang
Began when my bell rang.
The zero-hour started
When my permission was granted.
I set the universe in action,
Trillions of stars in attraction.

Life started creeping
After a long time of sleeping.
I started peeping,
Calling the people for regrouping,
A new era was sweeping,
For time was then leaping.

As starter, as organizer
And as multiplier,
I, the zero, put all together
In one centre,
Parading with each other,
And expanding at wish, further and further.

I became the digit from where
All things begin.
I am aware
The rest around my orbit spin.
I am the lucky number, I swear
That you will always win.

All the time, I am on call,
My name is known to all.
I am small,
I'm a fireball,
I reach any goal
If it is part of my role.

I don't sleep day or night,
Up, down, left or right.
You may or might
Catch a glimpse of my sight
In the darkness or the light
When the time is right.

By accident
I was found in the orient,
Collecting vital evidence
As part of a new net
Known as the Internet:
What a lovely coincidence!

See what I can do.
To list only a few,
I grew to be true
For you, you and you.
To give you a clue,
I am needed when you need rescue.

I never eat or drink:
I only think
With a blink.
I am ready to shrink
Any chink in a kink
Of any kind of rink.

That is why I am a crypto-digit:
Nothing in it,
Bit by bit.
All numbers benefit.
In my basket,
They nicely sit.

Loving all numbers
We all exchange orders
In digital manners,
Carrying banners
To future users
Of computers.

Against my will
I am called nil.
My preferred skill
Is to erase and fill
Any number on the bill,
Just at will!

Believe it or not
I am the naughty naught,
Mixing with the lot.
Everything I got,
Because I am a dot
On the spot.

Perceive me as a broker,
A stoker and a joker,
Who can enter,
Foster and torture
Any creature
In any corner.

Everything starts
When I say go.
Everything retards
When I say slow.
But you know
I am everybody's fellow.

Every mathematical term and function
Needs my attention.
The theory of creation
With its fascination,
Without my adulation,
Stays in oblivation.

To change negative to positive
You need a neutral junction to be active.
To give directive
You need to be creative,
Innovative and interactive.
You need me as your superlative.

All equations need me
My balancing act to be,
To evaluate and to see
The space and its mystery.
Scientists do agree
I am part of eternity.

Minus or plus
Don't make a fuss.
All of us can discuss
How figures are dubious
And wrong answers
Make us furious.

I am the logic,
I am the lyric.
Everything kick, flick
Or tick
Because of my unseen arithmetic.
I am zero the magic.

What is Deltaism?

In brief, Deltaism could be described as post-Cubism, but its flexibility has surpassed Cubism. Its flexibility is achieved through its simplicity. As the name indicates, the Delta is the building block of Deltaism.

The term Deltaism, itself coined by the author, derives from the mathematical method used by Newton for the calculation of infinitesimal figures.

The Delta is also the fourth letter of the Greek alphabet, symbolized by the triangle, a geometrical figure which is not static, but free perpetually to become other, utterly and infinitely convertible. The core of the concept of Deltaism derives precisely from this potentiality, which is also posited as a new meeting point for art and science.

Therefore Deltaism is, above all, seen as an interpretative instrument capable of changing the way with which we approach models, and, as such, it has to do with various forms of thought – from art to politics.

In the final act, Deltaism has also its own philosophy of synergizing *Threesomeness* in conceiving excellence!